REFLECTIONS

Past, Present, Future

Reflections: Past, Present, Future

Reflections: Past, Present, Future

By
Why Yet

Reflections: Past, Present, Future

Reflections: Past, Present, Future

Copyright ©2017 Why Yet

Poetry; Relationships; Love; Life

All Rights Reserved. No part of this book may be reproduced or transmitted in any form or by any means, electronic or mechanical, including photocopying, recording, or by any information storage and retrieval system, in part or in full without the prior written permission of the publisher or the author, except in the case of brief quotations with proper reference, embodied in critical articles and reviews and certain other noncommercial uses permitted by copyright law. For permission requests, please address Anitbeet Productions, LLC.

Published 2018

Printed in the United States of America

ISBN: 978-0-9969666-9-6

Cover and Interior Design by Why Yet

For information, address:

Anitbeet Productions, LLC

5837 Magnolia St

Philadelphia, PA 19144

Why Yet

Reflecting on why we do the things that we do in our adult lives is one of the hardest but most necessary things we must do for ourselves. Not reflecting on what hurts us and why we repeat negative patterns of behavior in our lives allow those negative emotions to take root like an oak tree and grow beyond our grasp. This is my journey of reflection. My goal is to be a beacon of hope for someone needing the strength to dig into their reflection…

Enjoy,

Markisha 'Why Yet' Bunn

Past ··· **Pg 11**

Invisibility ················· Pg 14

Release ··················· Pg 15

Child's Pose ················ Pg 17

Scars ··················· Pg 21

Time Ticking Away ······ Pg 23

Breathe ·················· Pg 25

Mirror Me ················· Pg 28

Daddy Issues ··············· Pg 29

Why Yet

My Father's Influence .... Pg 30

Spirit of Life .... Pg 31

Present .... **Pg 34**

Hopeless Romantic .... Pg 36

Zing .... Pg 37

Why Do I Resist? .... Pg 39

Passive Aggressive .... Pg 40

Say .... Pg 42

Yearn to Be Free .... Pg 43

Reflections: Past, Present, Future

Don't Box Me In
....
.... Pg 45

Moonlight Dance
....
.... Pg 47

Badass
....
.... Pg 48

Inspirational Purge
....
.... Pg 50

A Mother's Tears
....
.... Pg 52

Winter's Bite
....
.... Pg 53

In Love with Love
....
.... Pg 54

The Woman in Me
....
.... Pg 55

Accepting Me
....
.... Pg 57

Good Morning, Beautiful
....
Pg 59

Why Yet

Future
....
.... **Pg 60**

Fear
....
.... Pg 61

Swimming
....
.... Pg 62

Keep Fighting
....
.... Pg 63

Mariposa Memories
....
.... Pg 64

My Heart
....
.... Pg 66

Quiet Musings
....
.... Pg 68

Imperfection Perfection
....
.... Pg 69

Musically In-Tuned
....
.... Pg 71

Reflections: Past, Present, Future

Musical Lover .... Pg 72

Everywhere .... Pg 73

Relentless .... Pg 74

Who Am I? .... Pg 75

PAST

The past is only as dangerous as our minds perceive. Once we conquer the fear in our minds, our future immediately begins to brighten...

Lifting my head from my tear stained pillow, I glanced at the clock on my nightstand. Eyes singed and blurred from another sleepless night, I strained to read the numbers. Seven oh-five, the numbers slowly came into focus as reality sank in. I was going to be late for work if I didn't get out of bed now! Jumping up, I immediately had to sit down. The head rush from bolting upright dictated my movements. Crawling from the head rush and exhaustion, I made my way to the bathroom to get washed and dressed.

Glancing at the calendar on my way to the hallway I glimpsed the date – January 27th. Usually I take that moment to celebrate but I just didn't feel like it today. Two-plus decades since that fateful Super Bowl and my emotions are still raw and sore. I mean – how do you forget the birth of one of your children, repeatedly, year after year?

My goal for this year has been to 'just get over it' as many family members have so rudely suggested. Easier said than done. After all, he is my dad. No, he wasn't there to celebrate anything for me but like countless young women before me and many to come after me, it doesn't decrease the hurt...

Washing my face, I resign myself to act as though today is just another day. After all I do have to go to work, so I can afford to go to work – yes, my sarcasm has increased markedly over the years. Avoiding looking at my reflection in the mirror, to avoid the emotional shit storm waiting to bombard me, I brush my teeth and quickly turn to the shower adjusting my water as needed. A quick glance at the clock lets me

Why Yet

know to shake a leg because time is cutting awfully close to me being late this morning.

Hot, steamy, pressured water is exactly what I needed. And what I didn't need at the same time. My emotional dam burst, flooding into the stream of water, blending into the pulsing sound of cleansing...

Invisibility

Why do I feel invisible?

Unknown to the seeing eye.

What part of me needs healing

To allow me to soar, to fly?

How far back do I need to go

In search of those broken pieces?

I long to know how to glue them back

For my spirit to get back on track

To being me...

Why Yet

Release

I close my eyes

Imagining

The things I'd say to you

To clear the air,

Clear my head,

Clear my heart

And the words begin to flow

Faster than I can capture them

In my ink filled space

In my haste to visualize

The response in your face

But

The truth is

I'm no longer interested

Because the scabs on my

Emotional wounds

Have dried and

The tears in my heart

Have died

Reflections: Past, Present, Future

Waiting for you to

Understand

That I love you

Because you are my dad –

Not because of material

Things you had.

Because your flesh

Helped create me,

And your DNA

Helped shape me,

And you are a part of my history,

And

I just wanted you...

Why Yet

Child's Pose

Kneeling,

Face down

In a prayerful position

I remember to breathe.

Concentrating on emptying my mind so I can benefit from this stretch.

Yoga is meant to benefit the mind and body?

Help clear the mind so clarity can be gained?

Five minutes into the child's pose

I suppose it's been five, I've lost count

In the distractions of my thoughts I've been trying to clear

And that resistance is what's hurting me.

Resisting what surfaces in the quiet of my mind.

Hurts, tears, fears, shame…

Emotions I run from but need to face

Because they have taken up residence in my mental space

And I am tired of running.

Worn down and worn out from the mental marathon of keep away.

Reflections: Past, Present, Future

Child's pose... who named this pose anyway?

I kneel, face down a few moments more when calm covers me like a blanket

As memory after memory floods my mind with the thought, "they abandoned you. They didn't protect you. They discarded you..."

The litany of thoughts hit like bricks as each thought immediately attached itself to a memory that corresponded.

Tears, uncontrollable and warm, flowed in acceptance of my emotions and I felt release...

Why Yet

I sit at my computer, staring at the screen, willing it to give me a hint of where to begin writing. My mind is blank, and frustration is sitting at my shoulder – teasing me. The ideas that were free flowing during the night, interrupting my sleep, were nowhere to be found. "I should have written them down." I grumble out loud. Wisps of memory give me a tickle of what the core idea was about. Like that memory that dashes away when you focus your attention on it, the idea ran away just as I went to grasp it.

Walking away from the computer to grab some Cheetos from the kitchen, I hear the undeniable ping of an instant message. Ahh, good 'ole Yahoo! Messenger strikes again. I check the message as I sit back down, allowing the distraction to have my full attention. Glancing at the bottom of the computer screen, the clock reads 1:21 am. I know what this message is about, tsk, tsk.

As sure as sugar, I open the message and it's from some guy who 'happened' to see one of my poems in the group chat and he wanted to say 'hello'. His rehearsed come on reminded me of the idea I had struggled to grasp earlier…

Snatching my notebook open and flipping to a clean page I scribbled as fast as the thoughts would appear. As I wrote, I heard footsteps coming down the second-floor hallway. Knowing it was your father, because you were at work, I quickly shut the computer down, stashed my notebook in a bag of yarn and began cutting the lights off so I could sneak upstairs to my bedroom and close the door. My heart didn't stop racing until you came home from work in the morning...

Why Yet

Scars

These scars

Haunt me,

Taunt me,

Burn and hurt.

This pain shattered my heart

And crumbled my trust

But amidst the dust trail

Of pieces, I found me.

Tear streaked and beaten

But

Not ever broken.

In the pain of scars,

Comes the strength of healing...

Reflections: Past, Present, Future

I awake to whispered voices downstairs and slowly glance at the clock on the dresser to see what time it is. Twelve forty-five. In the morning. The kids are all asleep and the house should be quiet. I think about what day it is, Wednesday, because it's after midnight. So, who could be downstairs, at this time of the night, on a weeknight no less? I debate whether to investigate because I'm tired from cleaning and cooking all day and chalk it up to the Cambodian neighbor down the street – until I hear a female laugh. That is not his daughter. Wide awake now, I silently climb out of bed and open the bedroom door. The laughter has gotten quieter as though it moved further back in the house. Then I hear the basement door open and footsteps descending. Who in the hell is in my house, at this time of the night?

I lean over the banister to listen closer. I start down the hall, but the floor creaks and I freeze in place. I don't want to wake the kids or alert whoever is in here that I'm awake. So, I backtrack to my quiet spot and listen for conversation. I don't hear any. For a few moments. Then a soft giggle. And a moan...

Why Yet

Time Ticking Away

Emotions drained

Swirling down

Evaporating

In the heat of frustration

Amidst the lies and deceit…

Safety deposit boxes

Of receipts covering dates

And times your actions

Caused a part of me to die,

Not a physical death,

But an emotional one.

Slowly chipping away

At the asbestos filled window sill

Of your self-induced fantasy

Full of fogged windows

From the breath of half-truths

And manipulations

That you wanted me to believe,

But once that last drop of emotion

Reflections: Past, Present, Future

Cascades down the porcelain bowl

Swirling like a tornado,

Like a ghost –

I'll be gone.

Why Yet

Breathe

Deep

Breaths

I need to inhale

The fragrance of freedom

To cleanse my lungs

Of the stench

Your abandonment left me with.

Breathe,

Breathe,

Breathe.

I can't stop this stream of tears

Threatening to consume me in the confusion of why,

Why?

You were my template

From which I learned what to expect

As the hurt and pain of your absence

Consoled me on dark nights

With thoughts of why?

Why?

Reflections: Past, Present, Future

Breathe,

Breathe,

Feeling unprotected in a hostile world

Left to wander unguarded, uncared for

Wondering why?

Why?

Although I loved, honored and cherished

That which helped create me

I could not help feeling less than

Because he who made me,

Left me.

Why?

Why?

Breathe,

Breathe,

So many times,

So many tears

Fell on deaf ears for want of a father

Who knew not how to be there...

Why Yet

So many women today are unknowingly reliving their relationships with their fathers through different men and don't understand that the type of men we choose reflect some aspect of our relationship with our fathers (or lack thereof). This was a difficult one for me to face as I had tried to convince myself that I had 'gotten over' my father's absence... until I HAD to reflect on my relationships with myself and with others...

Mirror Me

Sadness and shame averts my gaze

From the glistening haze of the mirror –

Me.

I refuse to look in the face of the child

My father refuses to see.

Me.

Asking for permission to feel pretty,

To feel wanted,

And being left with an unfillable void.

Me.

Why Yet

Daddy Issues

I laugh,

Because it hurts to keep crying.

I dance,

Because the tears burn tracks along my face.

I sing,

So the angels can feel my pain and console me

I fear,

Because my heart does.

I feel,

Because disappointment has trained me well

And the spell of my daddy issues has found me.

My legs can no longer run.

My eyes can no longer hide

What my heart wishes were not true,

That I have daddy issues because he refused me…

Reflections: Past, Present, Future

My Father's Influence

The lack of your presence

Was present in my life

    Just look at my choice of men...

You set the bar for who my heart would yearn for,

    You.

As much as I tried to deny it, the truer it became.

Why Yet

Spirit of Life

My spirit of life is waning

Feeling the weight of my decision

To continue to love a man

Who isn't mine to love,

While being with a man who has not ever truly loved me.

The ripple of these decisions, are tearing me apart inside

Although I smile

And try to hide

The immense amount of pain

In my spirit of life

Asking God why?

Why would I feel this way about one, when I am unable to openly

Express these feelings?

Yet, how could these feelings be wrong?

The visual of his smile brightens my day

Knowing he is okay

But others would say my love for him is wrong anyway.

Reflections: Past, Present, Future

My spirit of life is dying inside

Crying because there is no way for my love

To spread its wings and fly free

Because my love for him

Consumes me

Knowing

He is not free to be with me.

Your smile sets me free,

Free to be me in all my quirkiness,

Free to be

Insecure in all my insecurities,

Free to be sensual and sexually all woman

You are the answer to my dreams before I fall asleep.

Why Yet

Too often, as women, we tend to overlook quite a bit in our quest to 'prove' our loyalty to our family, our friends, and even our significant other. I too, have done that for too long and for too many only to be left empty and exhausted and feeling used. On my journey, I have accepted that I am the one who deserves my loyalty first – before I can offer it to anyone else. I am the one who deserves my love first – before I offer it to someone else. Because once everyone else has what I am offering what will be left for me? When I am in need who will offer to be my rescuer? My cheerleader?

This journey is not an easy one. Many days I just don't feel equipped to do it. I feel as though I cannot take another step. I want to give up. I cry. I wish. I get angry because the road I have traveled thus far is not the road I envisioned for myself twenty years ago. The dreams I had for myself did not include having to revisit and dig up EVERY painful moment of my life and dissect it. But this is where my journey has led me so that I can continue forward. As painful as this leg of my journey has been, it has also been necessary to endure to share this with you.

Don't turn away if any of these words strike close to home. That is your spirit speaking to you because there is healing you must do. Don't ignore it like I did. Borrow my energy and face what you have buried. Dig up your Beloved and give it (whatever it is) a proper burial so that you can continue becoming the fabulousness that you are.

Present

All too often we neglect the gift of the present trying to correct mistakes of the past in anticipation of the future...

Why Yet

An unexpected message received with a buzz of the vibrate mode on my phone. Glancing away from my computer screen, I put down the timesheet I had been looking over and pick up my phone. The notification alerted me to a new text message, so I open it. I needed a break from my office work. Inside was a wish for a good morning as well as a reminder that I am a strong, beautiful woman who deserves nothing but the best in everything...

My fingers begin typing swiftly on my phone, giving thanks for the compliment and inquiring about the family... mannered generalities as my thoughts travel into an abyss I thought locked away for all eternal...

Reflections: Past, Present, Future

Hopeless Romantic

Fantasizing about you

Brushing my hair away from my face

With fingertips that set fire to my soul,

A flamed blush

Coursing through my veins

As thoughts quickly skate

South of the border of your waistband,

Mentally encouraging this inferno inside

To become contagious

And catch you like a whirlwind

Of Caribbean heat...

Why Yet

Zing

It was quick as a flash

Like lightening

And gone just as quick

But left an immeasurable ache in my spirit

A feeling I tried filling with others

Which left immeasurable pain in my psyche

Because of the zing that occurred for me a lifetime ago…

Reflections: Past, Present, Future

I sat down at my computer ready to write. Typed twelve and a half pages of scenes and dialogue. Began notes for my character development. Yet when I told him what I had been working on I was met with an angry, acidic countenance. Questioning why I hadn't done any writing for him? In a moment of creative joy, he dismantled it all out of sheer nastiness, degrading anything that I had worked on. In that moment – I stopped writing my story. I turned off the laptop, put away the notebook and never mentioned it again. The energetic eagerness to draw out the flow of narrative dried to a shallow husk after being met with such hateful energy, but I encouraged it by not challenging that nastiness. I fed it by not countering the filth and degradation that spewed from his mouth.

Now, I secretly work on creative projects in silence. No longer do I share excitedly as I once did. That voice is still there. His voice. It hasn't gone away even though he has long since stopped talking about it. Every now and again, he'll curse and shout, yet each time, I hide my pen and tune out. Unfortunately, it's the inner voice that has picked up his call...

Why Yet

Why Do I Resist?

Why do I resist myself?

A curious thing to think on

Childhood conditioning of rejection

Slams the brakes

On my forward momentum

Sputtering like the engine

Of a stick shift done wrong

I've waited too long

For permission, I won't receive

From anyone but me.

So,

Why do I resist myself?

I find an interesting article online and come up with an idea for a blog post and just as I begin to type up my thoughts on the topic I stop. Cursor blinking at me questioningly. Doubt creeps in whispering to me that my post isn't engaging enough. My topic isn't interesting enough. My post won't be read by anyone. That little voice of negativity is dangerous. Cunning, convincing and creatively deceptive...

Why Yet

Passive Aggressive

I stop then go.

Go then stop.

Sultry then timid.

Happy then sad.

Hurt then angry.

Quiet then loud.

Searching then discouraged.

Why the merry-go-round of emotions?

I am still digging for the root of it.

Reflections: Past, Present, Future

Say

The words I wish to hear are trapped in the back of my mind

Floating on the guitar riff

In an abyss of memories

That threaten to pull me into their undertow

Although I refuse to go,

Refuse to be dragged down by the insecurities of you...

LOOK AT ME,

Or better yet, don't.

Not now, nor when I walk out of your door for good.

The guitar riff plays

To the rhythm of my footsteps

Tired of tapping to your drum beat

In someone else's heat.

Why Yet

Yearn to Be Free

I

Yearn to be free.

Free to be me.

Completely in my me zone,

Untethered and wispy

Like the branches of a willow tree…

Swaying in my creative breeze,

Drifting in Calypso seas

Of words and music and me…

Reflections: Past, Present, Future

Sitting in the parking lot looking at the building, I sigh. I feel depression sinking in, every time I show up for work. The upbeat and hopeful energy I had when I began this position is gone. My energy feels drained each day when I show up. No matter how much work I complete, the catty power struggle for dominance I encounter, irritates the life out of me and I just want to be free...

Whenever I feel contained, restrained or restricted in any way I yearn to break free. I rebel in all sorts of ways and not all the time does it benefit me. Even when I express my dislike for restrictions, those around me mistakenly believe they can tame me. I am un-tame able...

Why Yet

Don't Box Me In

I will do for you,

Work for you,

Work with you,

Cry for you,

Cry with you,

Defend,

Promote,

Protect you

If you don't box me in.

Don't create a cage to place me in – I will break free.

Don't try to place restrictions on me – I will break free.

Don't try to control me – I will break free.

And once I am free of you…

Reflections: Past, Present, Future

Every little girl wants to fall in love and get married to her Prince Charming. I am no exception, even though I have tried for many years to convince myself that I wasn't one of them. I tried convincing myself that I didn't need to have the fantasy life projected onto girls from a young age, that you aren't a woman until you fall in love and have the magical proposal, with the dream wedding and fabulous husband and kids. I didn't want to believe in that fairytale because it smelled too much like Santa Claus and the Tooth Fairy. But the smell was enticing none the less. The alluring scent of maybe I could be chosen, like in the Golden Child. To be someone's chosen one seemed attainable, once…

The reality is, I choose me. Every day I wake up I have been chosen. I am choosing. As I write this, bleeding my pain onto these pages, I AM CHOOSING ME. Because I know what not being chosen feels like and it hurts like a bitch! So, every day I do something to remind myself that today, I CHOOSE ME. I am worth choosing because I am a badass Why Yet and you can't find another anywhere on this planet. So, when you feel down, like you are ready to take a handful of Fukitalls and give the world the finger, remember YOU ARE A BADASS (insert your name) and there won't be another one like you EVER!

Why Yet

Moonlight Dance

Thump, thump, thump

The drums call my heart out of its painful slumber

Scars from abuse, misuse and confusion have scabbed over

Slowing the rhythm of my life to a crawl.

The highway of bass clef awakens me,

The treble jars my emotions out of a catatonic state.

New life breathes into my lungs

Energizing,

Renewing,

Allowing me to review the hibernative state I had cocooned in.

Bright moonlit rays shine through the window

As the musical notes reawakens my senses

Allowing all to pour out onto the page

With the blood of my pen

As the words dance in the moonlight…

Reflections: Past, Present, Future

Badass

My reflection winks at me

When I get my eyeliner perfect.

My goals checked off

One by one

Has me feeling damn good.

Quality time spent with the little ones

And dinner in the oven.

Even the library books are returned on time

With school supplies on the horizon.

I am a badass

When I want to be.

Grown and sexy

When I'm feeling free

Because I'm a badass

So, don't mess with me.

The road I travel

Is graveled and rocky

But I walk it

With grace

Why Yet

        Like 5-inch platforms

        In Givenchy's place

        Because I'm a badass...

Reflections: Past, Present, Future

Inspirational Purge

My mind

Allows the thoughts free reign

To fly,

As my pen races to keep pace

With the rhythm of my emotions,

As the music plays in my ears

Reminding me of who I am

And how far I have come

Musically healing wounds

I desperately tried to hide.

Wounds that threatened a living death

Deeper than the blackest holes of hell.

The sweet silhouettes of music notes

Tossed a life line to my mental self

And rescued me

From a painful abyss of nothingness.

Why Yet

My mother is a very strong woman. Watching her as a child I didn't understand what she possibly could have been feeling. Now as a mother myself I understand the pain a mother feels when her children are in pain. As a woman, I understand the pain and frustration of an unwilling partner. I am learning how to navigate between the two...

Reflections: Past, Present, Future

A Mother's Tears

My mother's tears

Were not cried in vain

For I am her champion.

Knowing the pain of an unreturned love

I vow to heal her.

My mother's tears

Are my tears

Because her pain

Is my pain, a mother's pain, a woman's pain,

A burning pain

That

I vow to heal.

My mother's tears

Were not cried in vain

Nor were my own

Because those tears fed a determination

Unmatched by anything on Earth.

Why Yet

Winter's Bite

Crisp is the morning air.

Sun ablaze in the sky.

Wind whipping through my hair

Pulling tears from my eyes.

Spring teased us just a week gone by

With warm air and

Sun filled skies

Taunting us with promises

Although the calendar whispered *February*...

Reflections: Past, Present, Future

In Love with Love

I am in love

With Love.

For she delivered to me experiences

That shined light

On the beauty I exude to others.

Beauty I failed to witness within.

So, she wrapped my love

In a chocolate package

And proceeded to instruct me

How love behaves

In a way she knew I would accept.

He forever holds my heart…

Why Yet

The Woman in Me

Love flows as strong as a river current

Unrestricted by space, time or circumstance.

Once my heart opens, the woman in me

Flourishes,

Glows,

Grows,

And knows that pure beauty is a rarity in the world.

Peace flows as smooth as silken strands

Guided by love like a traveler wandering in

A golden desert,

Guiding,

Providing direction

And connection to the source of the peaceful flow…

Beauty is transcendent

Across space and time

Regardless of age

Like a wine ripening for the perfect celebration of life.

The heavenly river current of love heals and nurtures

Because of the woman in me…

Once I started on that journey of healing and self-reflection a lot of things began to change, starting with how I view my life. Patterns began to emerge, and I can see the bullshit for what it is. I don't fear it though and that's a good thing. Now I see what is wrong I can begin to fix it or walk away from it. At this stage of my life I am lacing up my shoes...

The best thing I have done for myself is reach out to other women for guidance. Women who have been where I am and who are where I want to be. I realized a long time ago that where I am right now is NOT where I want to be, but I am here because I neglected myself. I mistreated myself by accepting less than what I deserve. I accepted less than what I require for myself to maintain my happiness. No more will I do that to myself...

Why Yet

Accepting Me

This is me.

I am who I am and that's alright.

Aquarian beauty

In all my light

Shining, glistening, glittering…

I've accepted less

Only out of a need to bury the hurt of my past

Only for a mighty oak of pain to grow

And splinter the sidewalk of my happy street

Dropping acorns of thorn covered aches and pains

In my path at every step…

I'm accepting me

With my faults draped in velvet tears

My mistakes covered in crocheted blankets

Warmed with the broken promises of past loves…

I'm accepting me

As I am

Fully,

Immersed in my cleansing,

Reflections: Past, Present, Future

Tears rinsing the blood

From my broken heart and bruised ego,

Allowing myself to emerge free.

Free from obligations to anyone but me.

Free to feel the breeze blow my locs

And caress my face as I chase my dreams...

Why Yet

Good Morning, Beautiful

Good morning, beautiful.

Look at me.

I am you

And we are here, together.

Scars and all.

We are always

One and the same

Twin flames

Of the same candle

Looking for clarity external, but…

The clarity has always been within us.

Scars and all…

Good morning, beautiful.

I am you.

Future

The future is unknown to us but open to our hearts desires and efforts towards those desires. Keep striving forward...

Why Yet

Fear

You tried to bind me,

Wrapped my mind in blankets

Of how bad it could be,

Wrapped in silicone layers

Of a warped existence

Strengthened by my own ignorance.

Fear,

You did your job to perfection,

Crippling me mentally

Through my own inaction.

Well played.

But now, Fear,

I recognize you for who you are...

A distractive mosquito

Trying to disturb the paradise that is my life.

Reflections: Past, Present, Future

Swimming

Cool, crisp waves carry me along

Floating on the current of a distant memory

That leaves me feeling...

A myriad of emotions

A torrent of

Love, angst, and anxiety

Blended together,

Swimming along in my mental cortex,

Backstroking through my thought process

Interrupting my careful plans of forward movement...

Why Yet

Keep Fighting

It hurts.

It's okay.

The road is rough

But keep going your way.

Not everyone will understand

The road you travel

As they shouldn't

Because this is your journey.

It hurts.

I know,

But by and by

Watch how you grow

Through the pain,

Deceit, and insincerity…

Remember growth comes through pain,

Gain comes through strain

When you keep fighting…

Reflections: Past, Present, Future

Mariposa Memories

Struggle, strain, resistance

Heartache in the distance

As the barrier cracks...

A sliver of light,

Refreshing and bright

Offers hope and a promise of more

Simplistic happiness

But the darkness is reaching,

Memories of tears fresh falling pain.

Hurts from before, and then

Another crack.

And another.

I stretch toward the light

Cracking more of the barrier and pieces fall away

Welcoming in a warm flood of rejuvenating light

And I can fly free...

Why Yet

Who am I? Who do I want to be? What makes me happy? Who enhances my happiness? Where do I want to be? These are the questions that urged me to reflect on me. To sit quiet long enough to hear the answers to these, and other questions. Simple questions yet very powerful when I have been hiding and running from myself for so long. The time has come to stop running and face that which scares me most: Myself.

Reflections: Past, Present, Future

My Heart

My heart...

Is an open chasm, unto which I bleed

The colors of Aquarian love...

Vibrant hues of violets and blue

Vibrating at a fiery pace

Mimicking the flutter,

The breezy pitter-patter of wings

My heart...

Is a dungeon of memories

Stored away with shadows

Of love given and not returned

Looking for a home,

An adoptive touch,

A comforting stare

Into soulful eyes like my own but...

My heart,

Still beats

Rhythmically,

In time to the drum of my other spiritual part,

Why Yet

My cosmic companion

Who still seeks the matching thump to his beat

And as I apply my Red Cross patch of healing

I feel stronger,

As the breath of creativity

Increases the flow of my positive energy…

Reflections: Past, Present, Future

Quiet Musings

"I love the sound of your voice..."
Trails across my memory at the most
Inopportune times,
Creating a barrier to productive concentrations
Eliciting responses unsuitable
For the work place.
Broadcasting other memories
In response,
Creating a ripple effect that stirs
Warmth and a tightening of muscles
In regions within...

Why Yet

Imperfection Perfection

Staring at my reflection,

At the results of bearing life.

Stretch marks gracefully swim

Across my abdomen in waves

Of caramel kisses.

The low slope of my breasts

Reflect the nourishment

I provided for all who came forth

From my body.

My body is imperfectly perfect

In its own way,

Loving me as I love it...

Many days when I struggle with wanting to 'adult' I turn on music and allow the energy of the rhythmic notes to sooth me. Getting lost in the songs helps me to realign my thoughts and clear away or face whatever thoughts has me feeling moody. I love music and I always have. Music encompasses pure emotion and renders words unnecessary, sometimes…

Why Yet

Musically In-Tuned

Smooth notes musically entwined

Tickling my heart strings

With lyrics laced

In love…

The bass rumbled through my body

Like the steel drums of Jamaica

Vibrating to a musical plane

Rattling my rib cage…

Musical Lover

Sensuous notes float away

From the ivory keys of the piano

As the drum beats in resonance to my heart

Creating colorful images of beauty

And peace

Within my mind's eye

Crafting peace in my heart

Swelling wide

As your voice

Lulls me into a lover's slumber…

Why Yet

Everywhere

The violin strings sing a soft song into my heart

Caressing the love that lives within

Softly stroking the nape of my neck

Like a gentle lover

Reuniting after a long absence,

Whispering the beauty of the moon in my ear

Melting the sadness

That formed around his absence...

Relentless

My thoughts race

As though fire is set to my mind's eye

Searing heat melding and fusing ideas

And images together

While reality threatens to tear them apart

But my journey is relentless,

The passion to find me

Is never ending,

Undying,

Always trying

To balance out my heart and mind

In space and time

While

Living

Relentless...

Why Yet

Who Am I?

Purple-esque hues,

Soft notes drifting across my ears.

Melodies rocking me,

Drifting me into a peaceful reverie,

Subduing my mind

Into the subsequent rhythmic bass

That quiets everything…

Why Yet? Why not? I am Why Yet. Passionately poetic and understanding of many things. I have come quite a way from where I used to be and for that I am grateful. Remembering to look at how far I have come versus how far I still must go is a chore, but well worth the effort. Some days are easier than others, but the great days are awesome, and I can look back on them and smile when I need a pick me up. These words were crafted over coffee, in my dreams, in the shower, at work, on route to work, during dinner, etc....

The inspirational women I have met so far on my journey have been the best. Even when they don't realize it. Thank you. For my parents, who shaped me through their experiences – thank you. I wouldn't be the woman I am today without all my experiences. For my past loves... thank you. You know who you are. Through the smiles and the pain, I have learned so much from each of you. For my future love, find me. These words are clearing my mental and emotional clutter and I'm donating the baggage to make room for you. For my social media followers (including Idris Elba – squee!) thank you for staying tuned in to me. I appreciate you.

For all who may be struggling with understanding the romantic choices in your life, just sit quietly and reflect on yourself. You'll be amazed at what you may learn! You are fearfully and wonderfully made.

Thank you for purchasing this book and trusting that you would enjoy my words. I only ask that you leave a review and share this book with someone who may benefit from it.

        Love Always,

           Why Yet

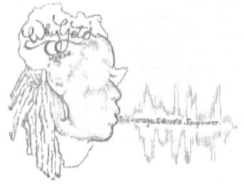

Reflections: Past, Present, Future

Other works by Why Yet:

Entangled Hearts (Available on Amazon.com)

Other works by Why Yet as Markisha Bunn:

Entangled Hearts (Available on amazon.com)

SIPS (Available on Amazon.com)

To follow Why Yet on social media:

Facebook: @whyyet.author; @why.yet;

Instagram: @why.yet

Twitter: @why_yet1

WordPress: whyyetswords.com

For questions, to order autographed books, booking for events send requests and inquiries to: markishabunn@gmail.com

Thank you for your purchase of this book and your support of the arts!

Warm regards,

Why Yet

Why Yet

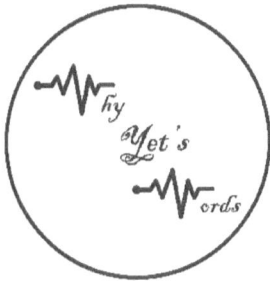

Reflections: Past, Present, Future

www.ingramcontent.com/pod-product-compliance
Lightning Source LLC
Chambersburg PA
CBHW020430010526
44118CB00010B/510